CRAZY CONCEPT CREATURES

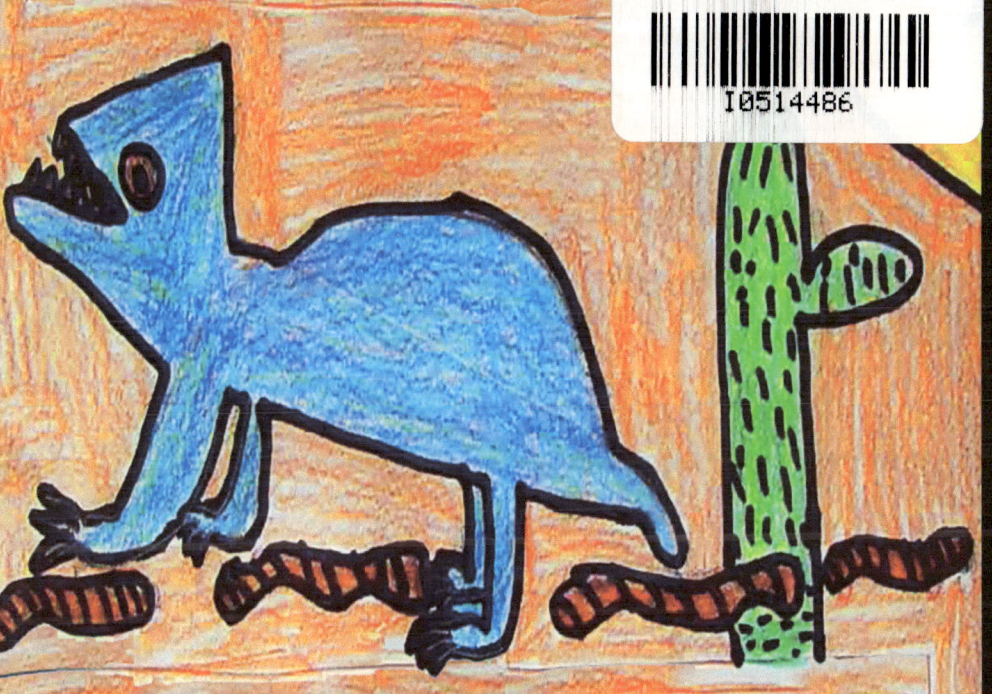

BY:
HENRY JOHNSON CHARTER SCHOOL
4TH GRADE SCHOLARS

Cover Design By:
Luisah-Mia
Diaz-Pereyra

Title Page:
Mercy Nyemah

Copyright 2021
HJCS Scolars
ISBN 978-1-7947-0441-1

Edited by Mr. Shaw

MAGMA SHARK

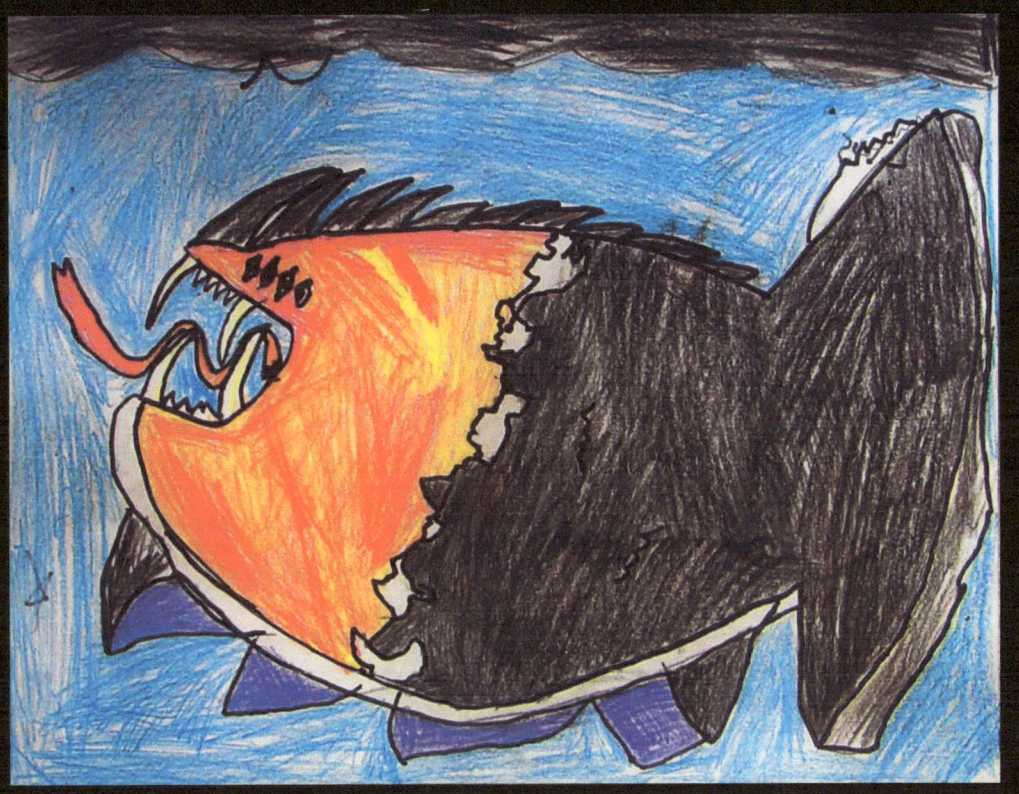

The Magma Shark is one of the fiercest sharks in the world. This dangerous predator lives in a mysterious place in the ocean. It moves with its giant fins and tail and it is as fast as a cheetah. It only eats the Great White Shark, even all of its bones.
The Magma Shark has long, sharp teeth to catch its prey and the spikes help protect it. The long tongue grabs the sharks and pulls them in.
Created by: Elijah Franco

AMERICAN GLIDER

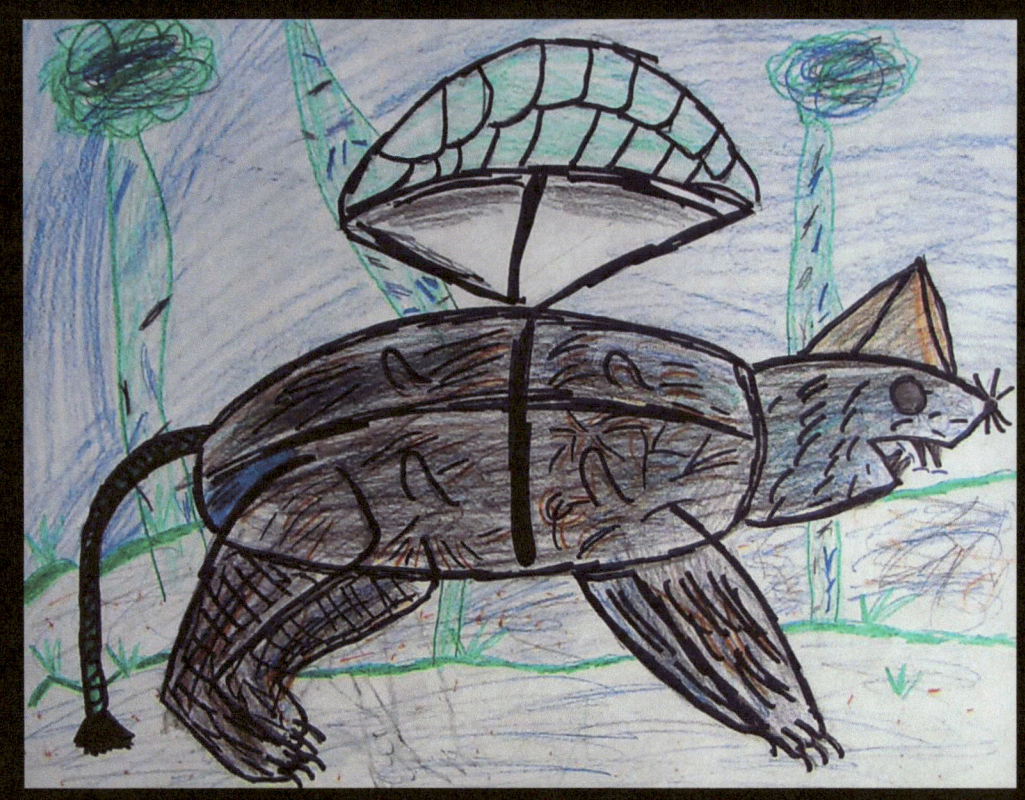

The American Glider is a fierce, strong creature. It can glide from tree to tree and it can eat anything. The American Glider lives in a mysterious jungle where nobody can find it. This creature moves with its skinny, fast legs and the glider on its back. This creature eats anything, even poisonous animals. It is most likely an omnivore. The American Glider's special body feature is its hard glider.
Created by: Kareyliz Vazquez

JUNGLE TIGER SNAKE MILLIPEDE

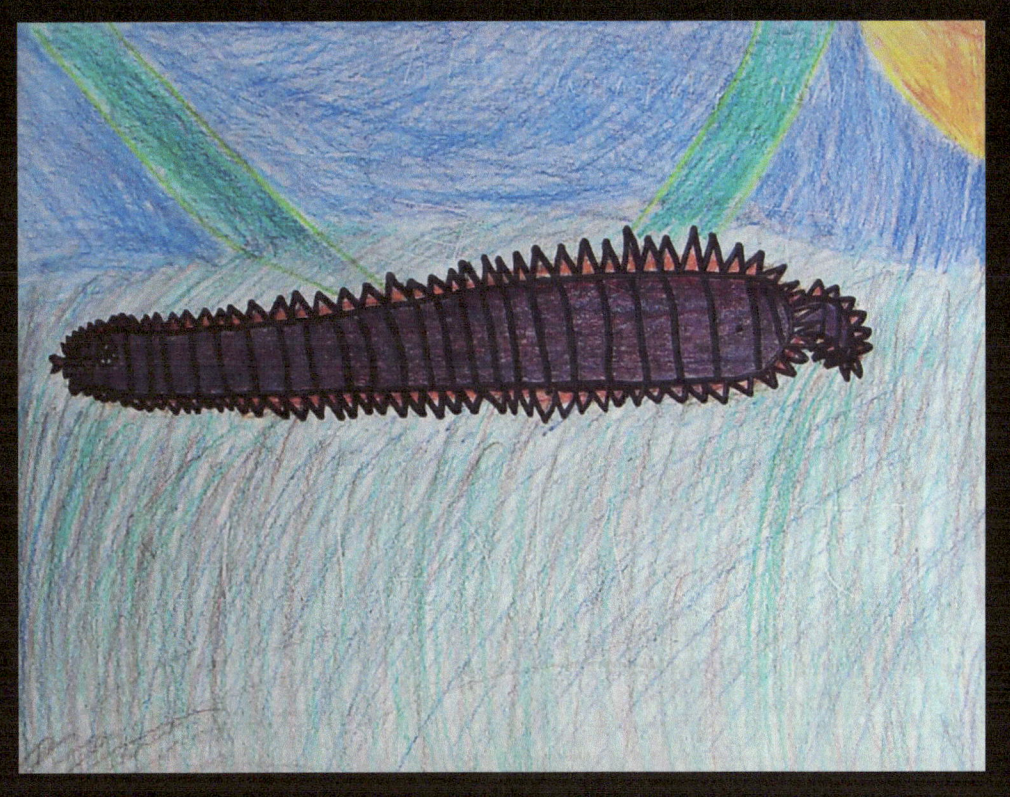

The Jungle Tiger Snake Millipede is a very astonishing insect. This smart animal lives in the jungle. This fast crawling creature moves with its short, pointy legs. This slow-eating insect eats snakes and it gets the snake with its pointy red legs. This creature has dark, rough poisonous skin and its predator is the American Glider.

Created by: Mercy Nyemah

FROSCORTIDEMO FROG

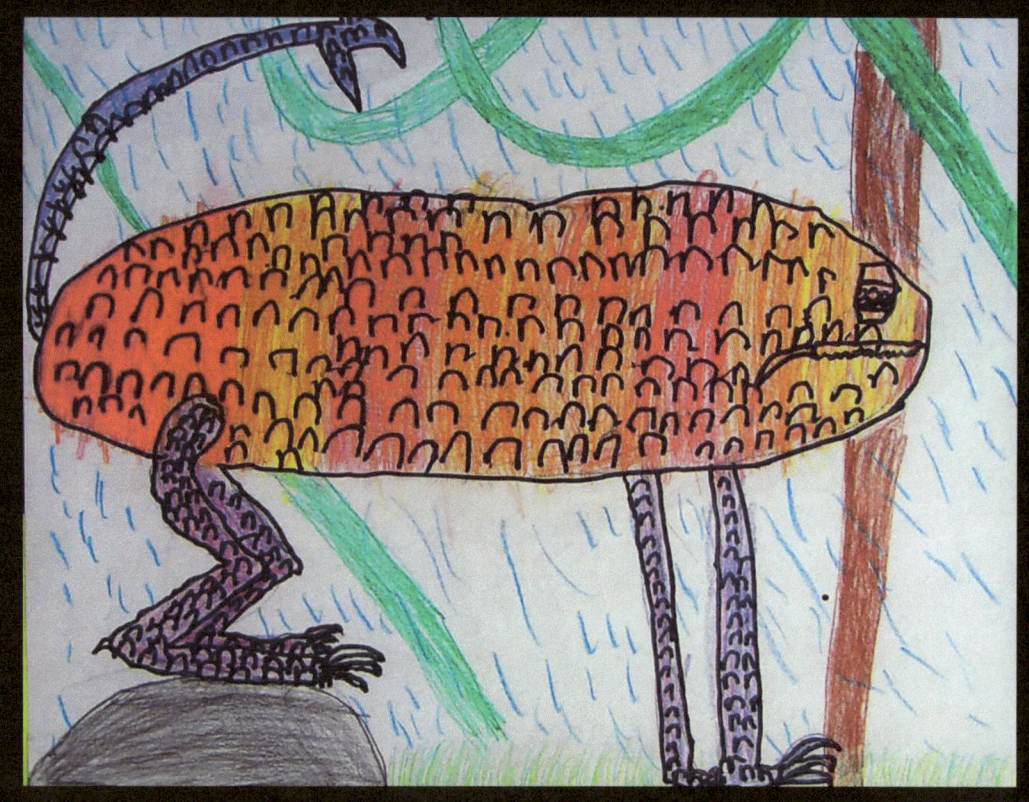

The Froscortidemo Frog lives in the forest. It's four feet tall and ten feet long. The Froscortidemo Frog oozes poisonous liquid The Froscortidemo Frog has claws with poison. Also, if it gets poisoned by another animal, it takes the other animal's poison and uses it for itself.

Created by: Damani Wilson-Anderson

BLUE RASPBERRY WOLF

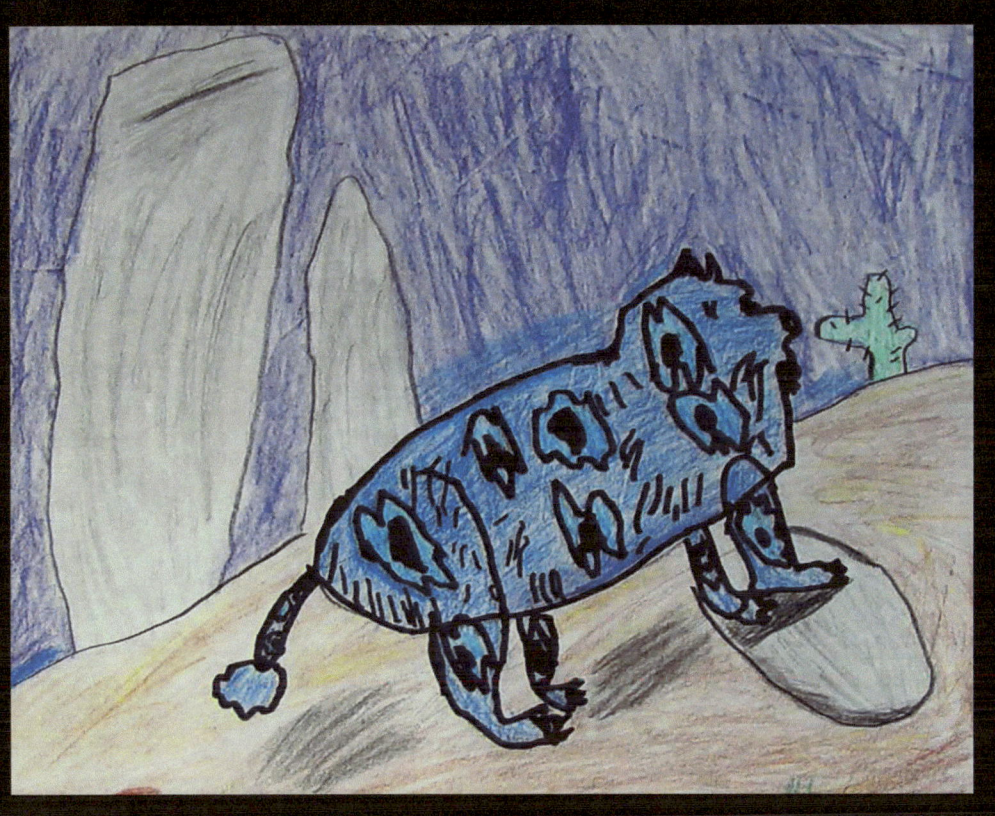

This creature is the Blue Raspberry Wolf. The Blue Raspberry Wolf lives in the desert. It has sharp claws and large, wide paws that stop it from sinking in the sand. It can run faster than a jaguar.
It eats smaller animals with its sharp teeth and claws. Its blue spots help it blend in with the plants.

Created by: Mya Daniels

SYNC BLUE

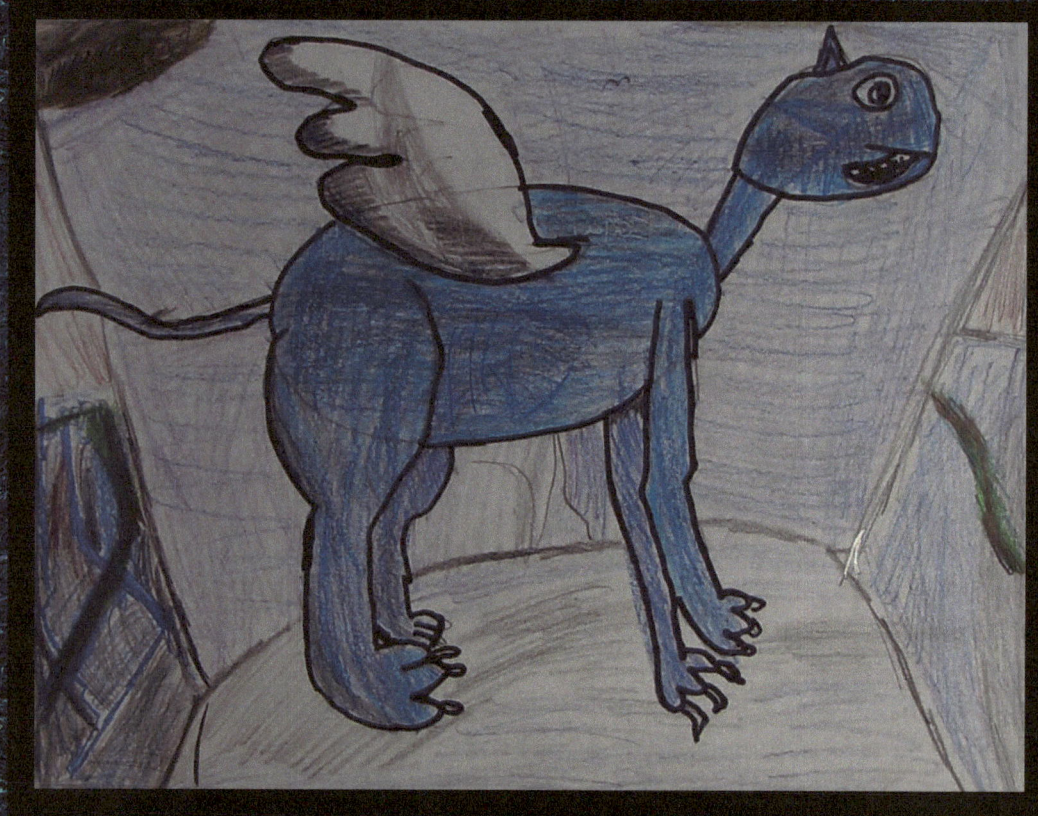

The Sync Blue is a very smart animal that is also sensitive.
The Sync Blue lives in the creepiest and deepest mountains. The Sync Blue flies and crawls. The Sync Blue eats the Poisonous Blue-Winged Panther along with fish, goats, and birds. The Sync Blue is immune to poison so it can eat the Poisonous Blue-Winged Panther.

Created by: Edgar Bautista-Sanchez

MIRAHPOLUSSKELD

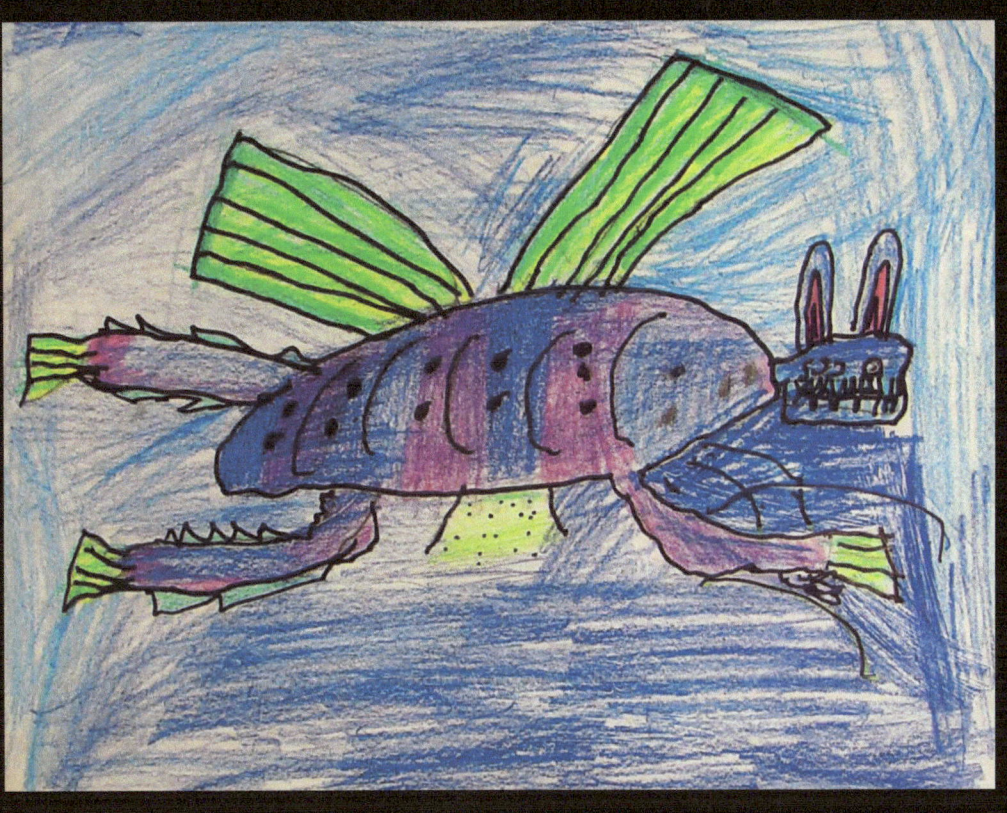

The amazing Mirahpolusskeld is a very abnormal creature. This creature is native to an extraordinary ocean. This creature swims with its wings and webbed feet. They flap away the water to help it swim. It eats a creature called a Danger Trap and it also eats plants. Three amazing, astounding, and extraordinary features it has are sense receptors, poison spikes and also a beam/ray that lifts its prey up.
Created by: McKinley Anderson

MIX SHARK

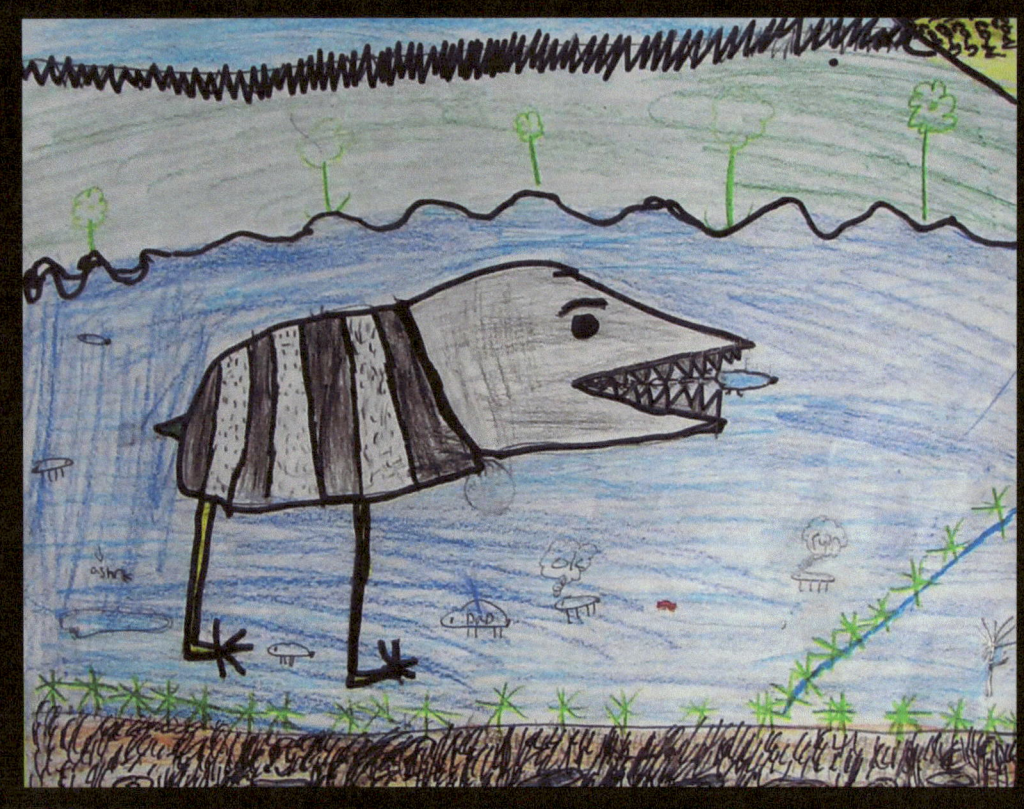

The Mix Shark is a creature that loves to eat humans. The Mix Shark lives in the ocean and eats all day long.
It moves with its duck feet. If something bites off its feet, the feet can grow back. The Mix Shark also eats fish. The special thing that the Mix Shark does is drink blood.

Created by: Nyanna Vega

RED HEADED BUNNY

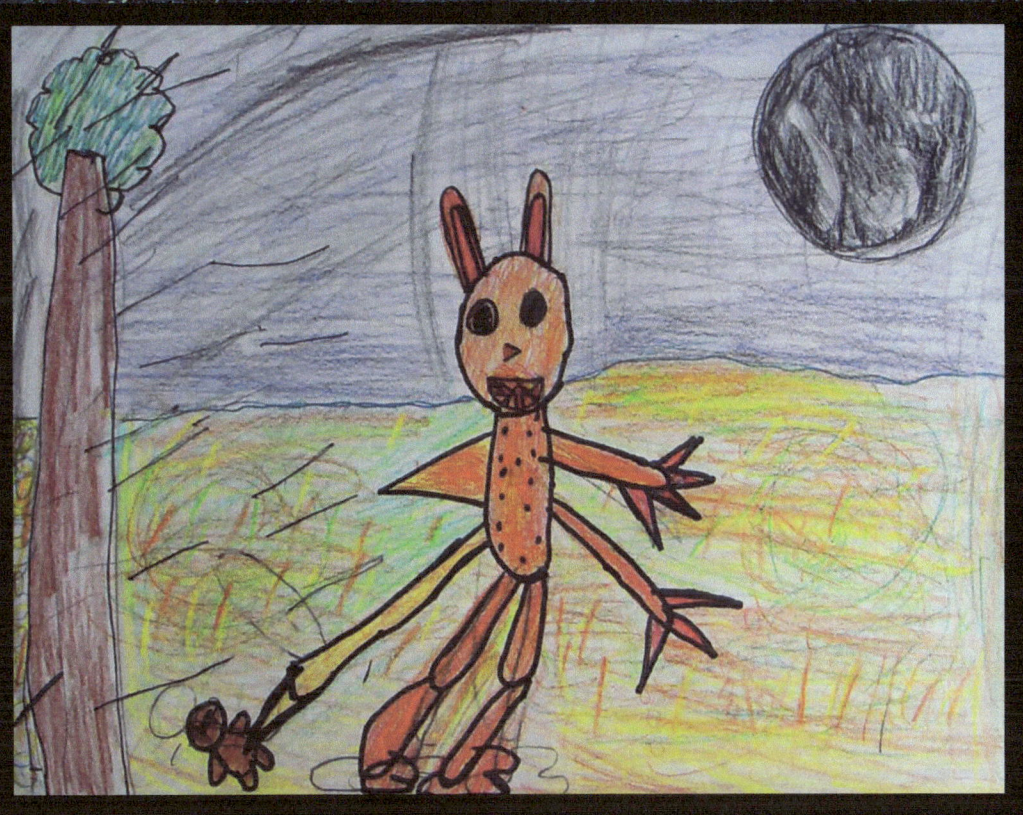

The Red Headed Bunny has a fin for throwing at its prey. The Red Headed Bunny lives in the grasslands and throws its fin to cut the grass so it can see its prey. It runs fast with its long legs and it can also teleport. The Red Headed Bunny eats small animals with its retractable claws. Another special feature is its tail which can stretch out to kill its prey.
Created by: Samuel Sylvain

DEEP SEA BLUE HUNTED SQUID

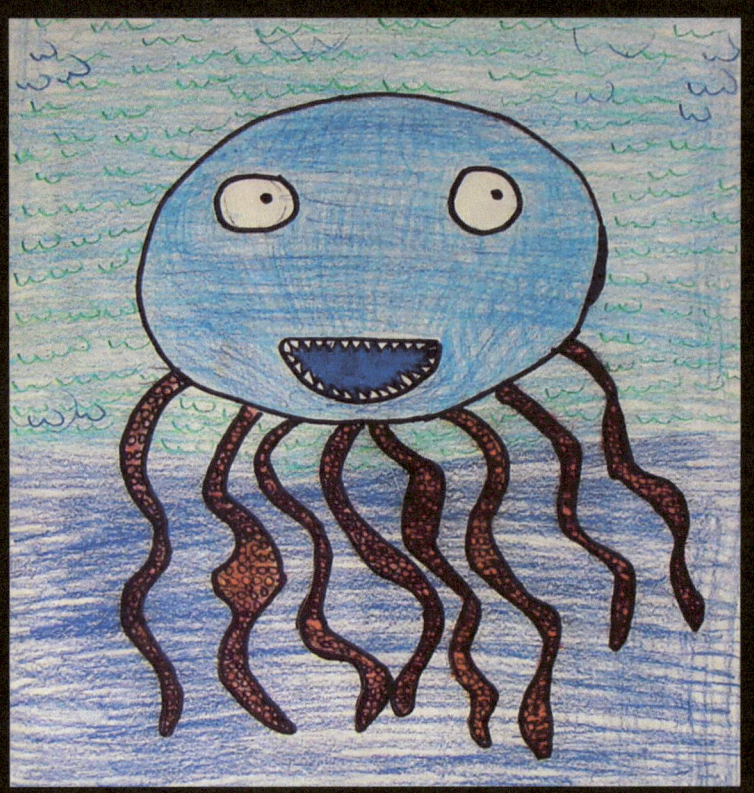

The Deep Sea Blue Hunted Squid is the most dangerous animal in the water. This creature lives in the ocean in the darkest parts. When it is ready to eat it goes into the light to find food. The Deep Sea Blue Hunted Squid has long tentacles and the creature's face is blue just like the ocean. This beast eats meat and other animals that look good to this creature. This animal has poisonous tentacles.
Created by: Leoney Sharpe

OTF

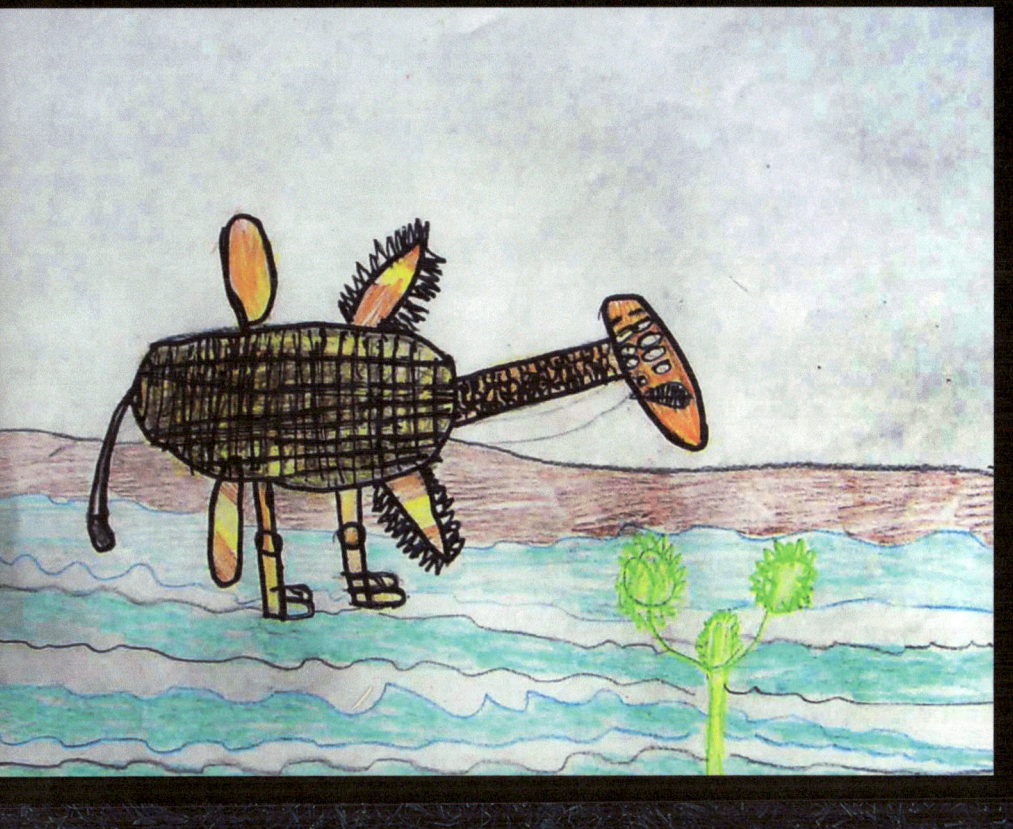

This animal lives in the air and the water. It moves with its two feet and wings. It has spikes on its wings. The sharp spikes and colors scare predators.
It eats fish and birds in the sky because it can fly. This creature's specialization is the wings and spikes.

Created by: Dahmel Bryce

SEVEN-LEGGED BEAR

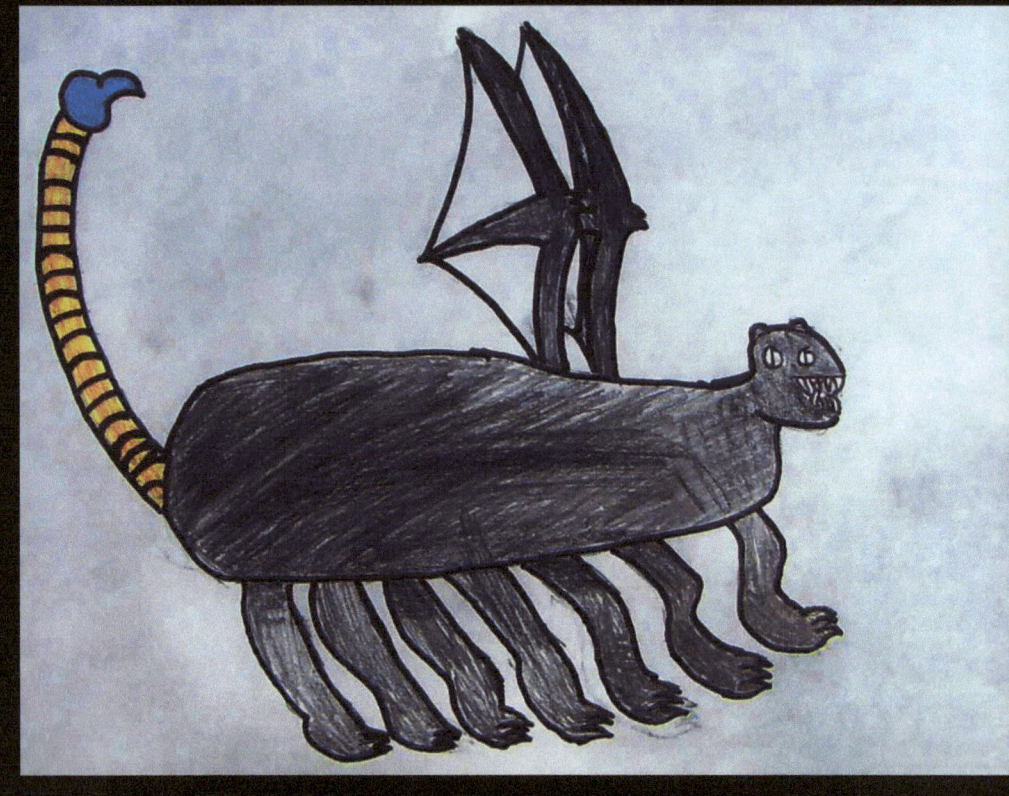

The Seven-Legged Bear is a predator with wings and sharp teeth. This beast lives in the cold arctic and it survives because it has thick fur. This creature moves by running with its long legs.
This animal eats seals, polar bears, and fish. One special feature it has is its poisonous tail that it uses to paralyze its prey.

Created by: Elijah Olarinde

POISONOUS FLYING FISH

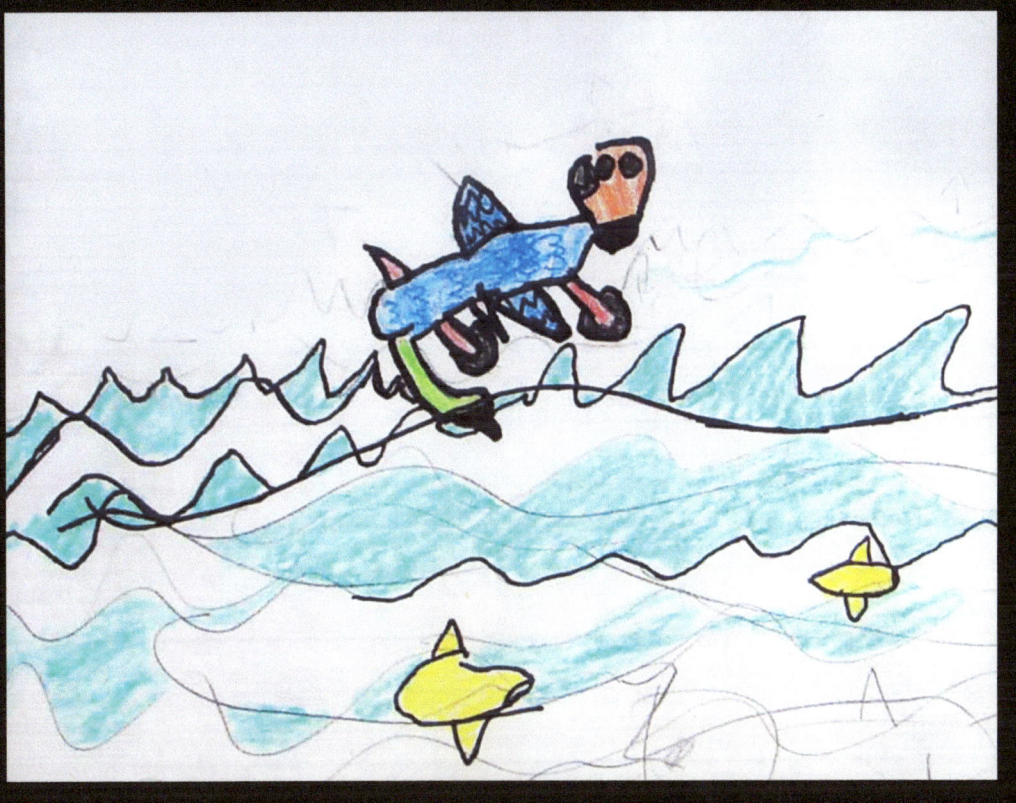

This creature is a Poisonous Flying Fish. This creature lives in the south. This creature moves with a special ability.
This animal eats plants. This animal's body has a poisonous tail that is retractable.

Created by: Qy'ir McCall

BLUE-WINGED TURTLE

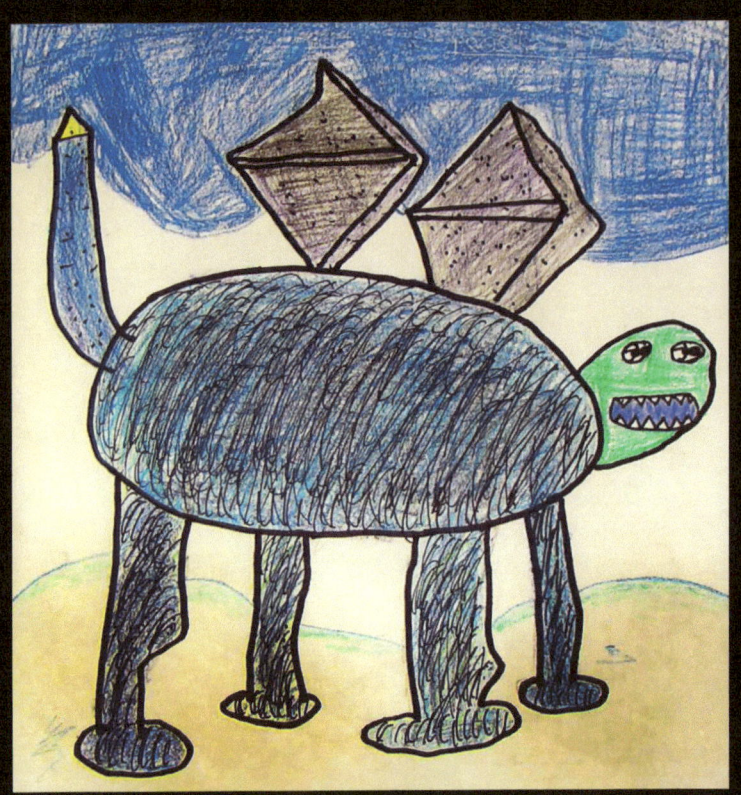

This creature is one of the biggest winged, poisonous creatures alive in the whole entire world. This animal lives in the cold, harsh, snowy arctic. This creature has a very hard body so you can't bite through it and a poisonous stinger. It also has fur on top of its hard skin. Also, it has a specialized tail to attract its prey with a bright stinger. This animal can walk on its long, thick legs and fly iwth its big bat wings.
This animal eats large prey. Some adaptations it has to help this animal eat is that it stings its prey and can fly away if something tries to attack it.
Created by: Daomi Chevannes

GREEN MEAT EATER

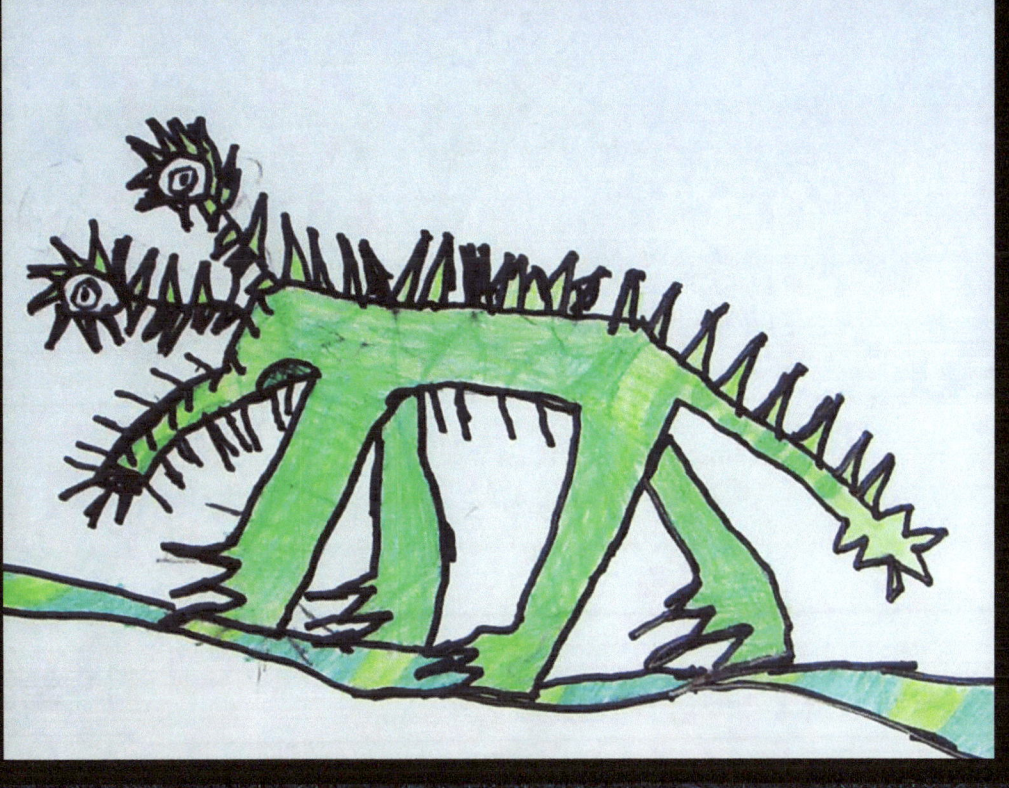

The Green Meat Eater is a good survivor that lives in the grasslands. This animal moves at a stealthy, slow pace. This animal lives in a dry, grassy biome.
This animal eats meat with its sharp, pointy teeth. It uses its tail to stun its prey.

Created by: Brayden Flower

SNOWY GIRAFFE

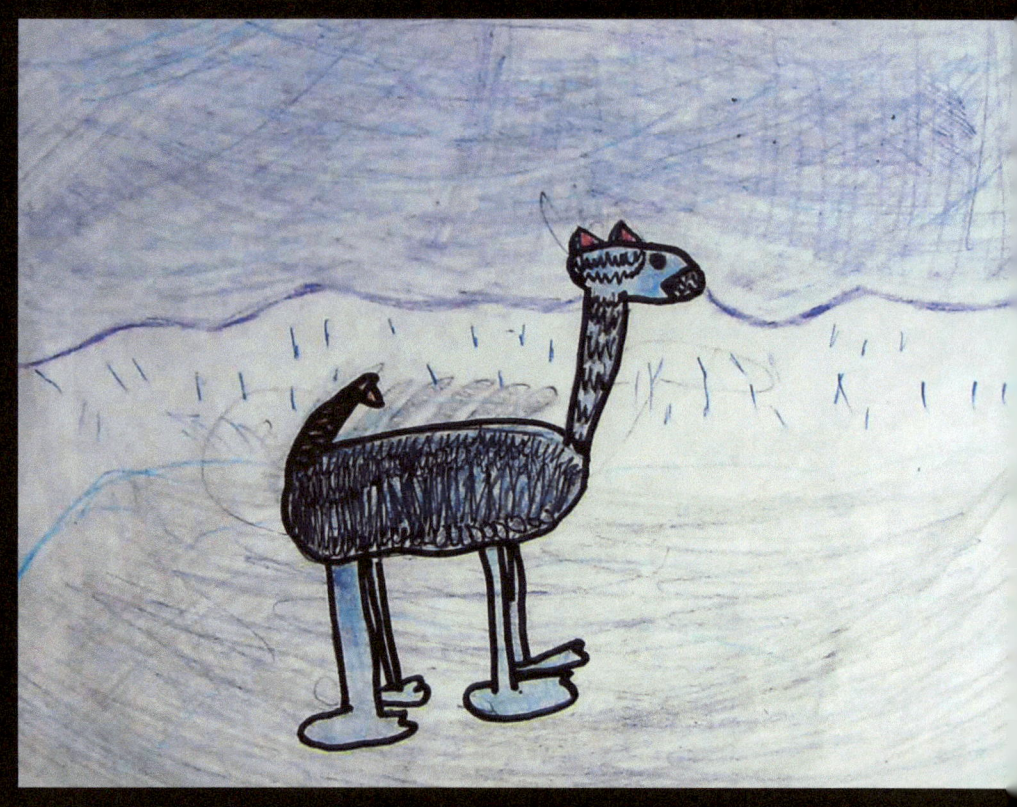

The Snowy Giraffe is a specialized creature that lives in a snowy environment. This creature lives in the arctic. It has big feet to help it not sink in the snow.
The Snowy Giraffe eats meat with its sharp teeth. A special body feature that this creature has is that it has a stinger to stab its prey with.

Created by: Luisah-Mia Diaz-Pereyra

DARK KNIGHT PANTHER

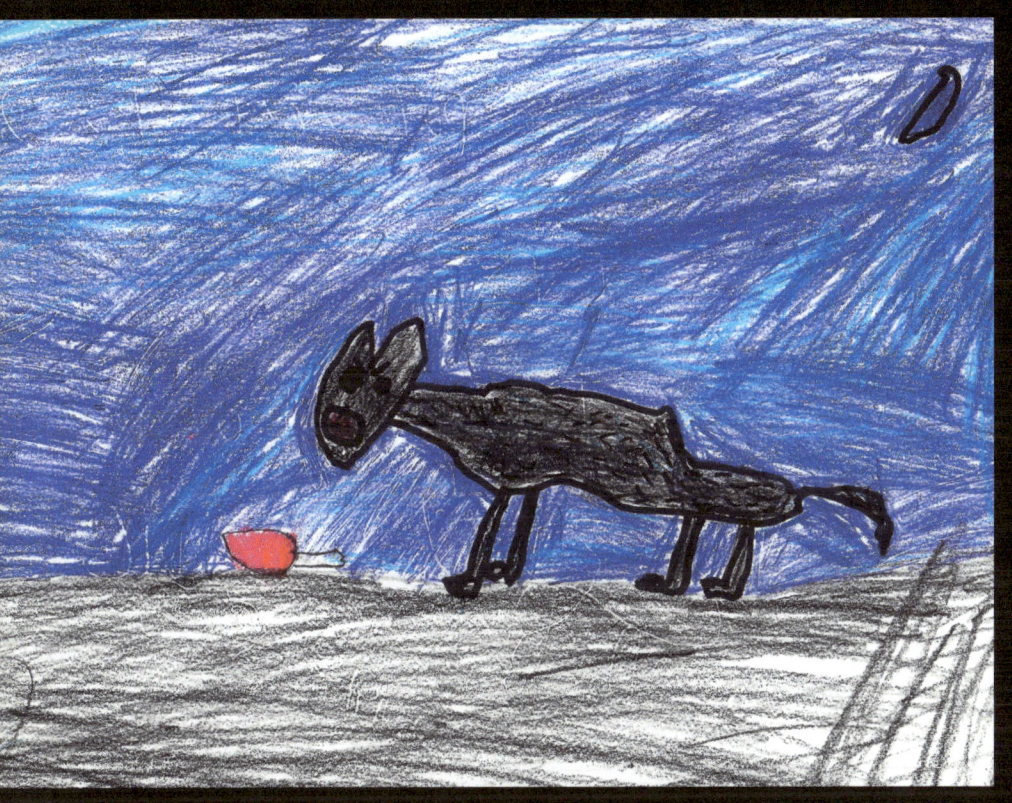

The Dark Knight Panther lives anywhere in the world. It has dark skin that helps it hunt in the dark and its eyes have night-vision. In the dark it looks completely invisible. This fearless Dark Knight Panther has no fear and is feared by other animals. This night dwelling creature moves at 100 miles per hour. It moves silently, but loudly when it wants.

Created by: Ishmeal Nelson

CUTE KILLER (Baby Form)

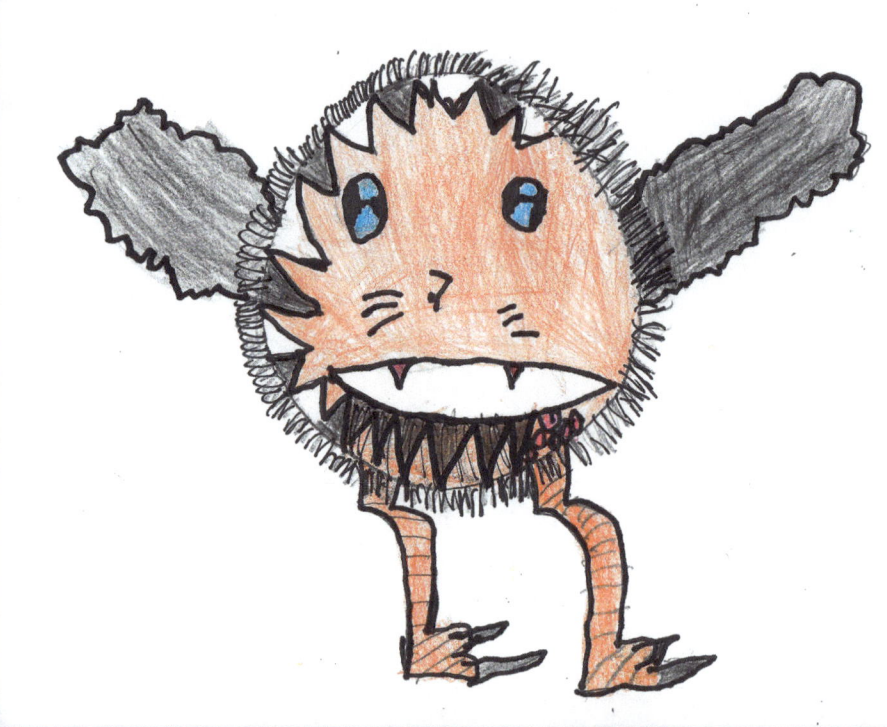

The Cute Killer (Baby Form) is perfect for the grasslands and barely dies until they get older. This creature dwells in the grasslands and hot places. It moves by flying when it is not a grown adult, but it changes the way it moves while it gets older. It eats meat and people, and their favorite food is the Walking Death Strider, but it better be cautious because that is one of its predators. The special body feature is its wings that it hides behind its back. It acts very cute in front of its dinner but then goes in for the strike!
Created by: Yannick Mugisha

CUTE KILLER (Adult Form)

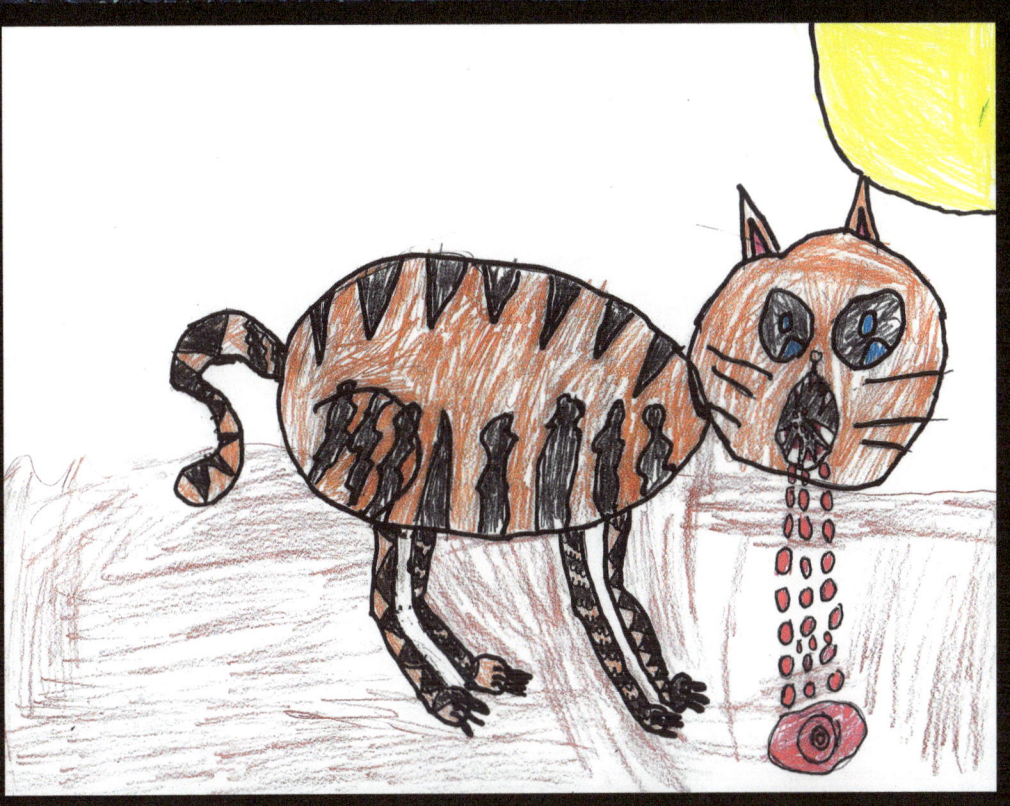

The Cute Killer (Adult Form) is perfect for the grasslands and it stays with its calf. This creature dwells in the grasslands where it is dry and it has lots of prey. This very deadly creature moves with its long legs which help it run up to 70-100 miles per hour. This cute but deadly creature eats deer, zebras, horses, cheetahs, and also the Walking Death Strider.

Created by: Kie'mhi Perkins

WALKING DEATH STRIDER

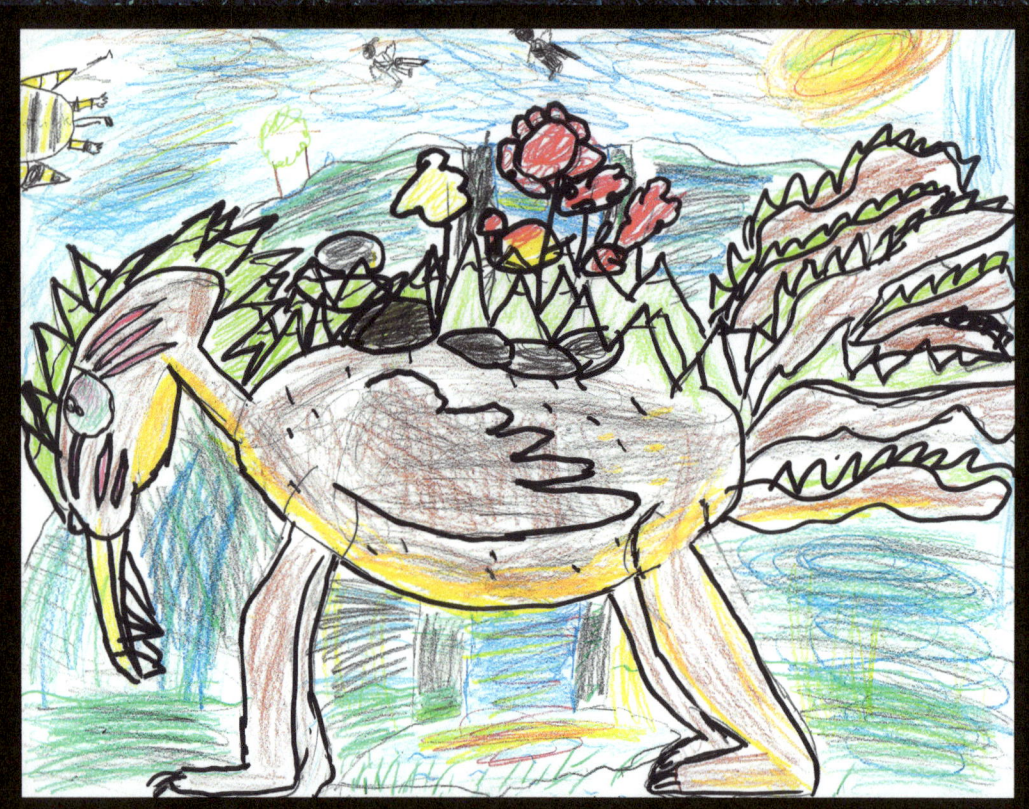

The Walking Death Strider is perfect for the forest and jungle. It sleeps in the ground. It is faster than a cheetah when speed walking, when it's running it moves at 90 mph, when flying it moves at 900 mph and can swim 1,000 miles per hour. It eats tigers, cheetahs, cows, birds, also the Beedactyl and the amazing Cute Killer. Its body features are its tails and posionous spikes that it can shoot out of its back and tails.
Created by: Brandon Barnes

BEEDACTYL

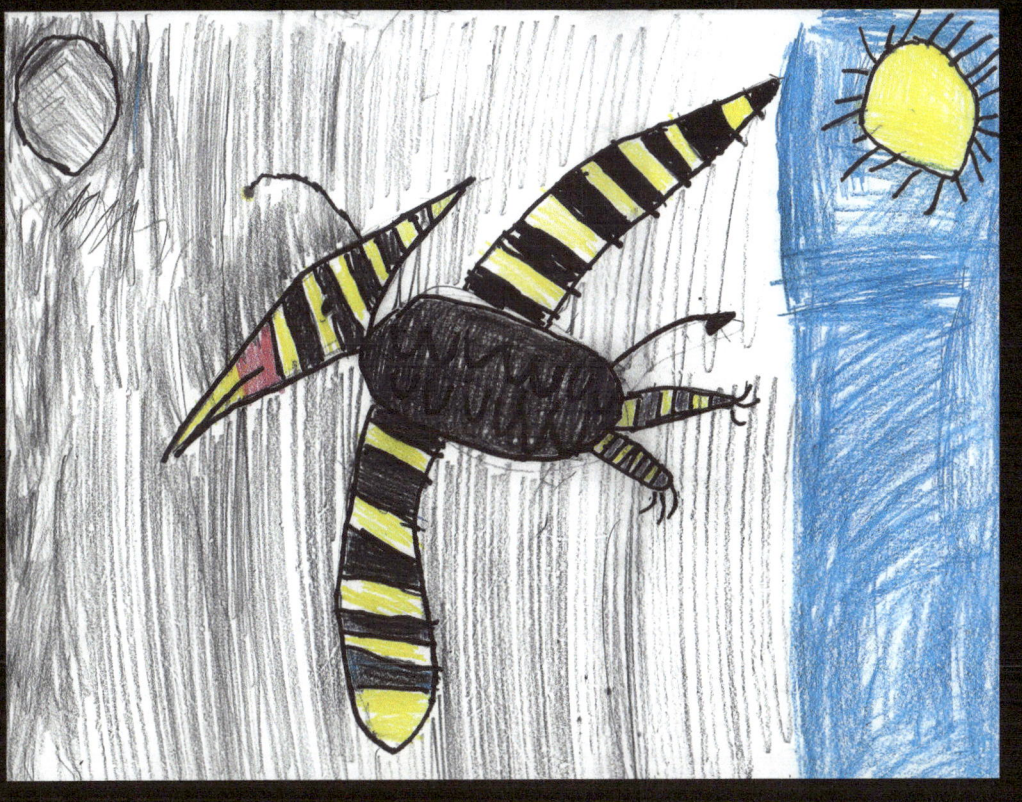

The Beedactyl looks like a be and it is fast. It is hunted by the Walking Death Strider. This creature lives in the jungle and in the forest. This creature flies through the air at 200 miles per hour to get away from its predators. This creature eats birds, bunnies, spiders, and other insects. This creature has a light on its head that it uses to attract insects more easily.
Created by: Tyrome Wallace

BANCHI

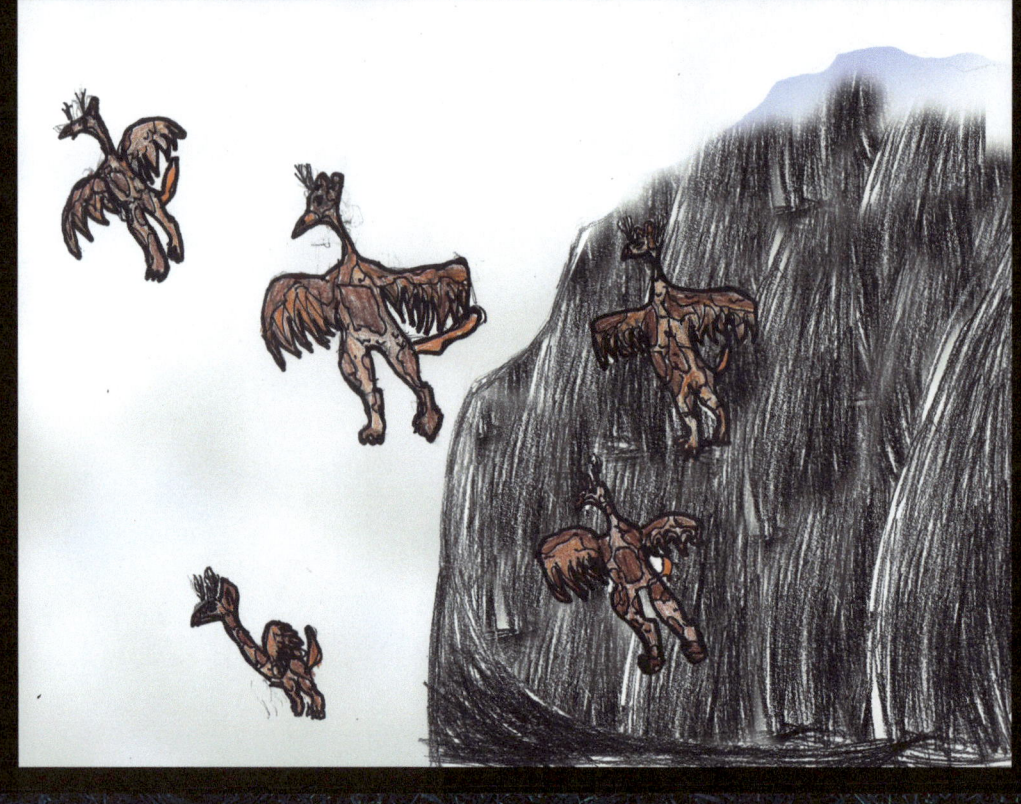

The Banchi is an amazingly well adapted creature to the mountains. This creature dwells on the highest peaks of the mountains. It also has the capability of living in colder areas. The creature usually flies, but it will rarely run or walk on the ground. The Banchi highly enjoys eating the plants it can find, but if meat is easy to spot, the Banchi will most likely eat it. This creature has retractable teeth. The teeth are hidden because of its beak. The animal's adaptation against predators is hitting areas that aren't protected. The Banchi flies at an astonishing 88 miles per hour.
Created by: Aileen Awah

NIGHT MOON PANTHER

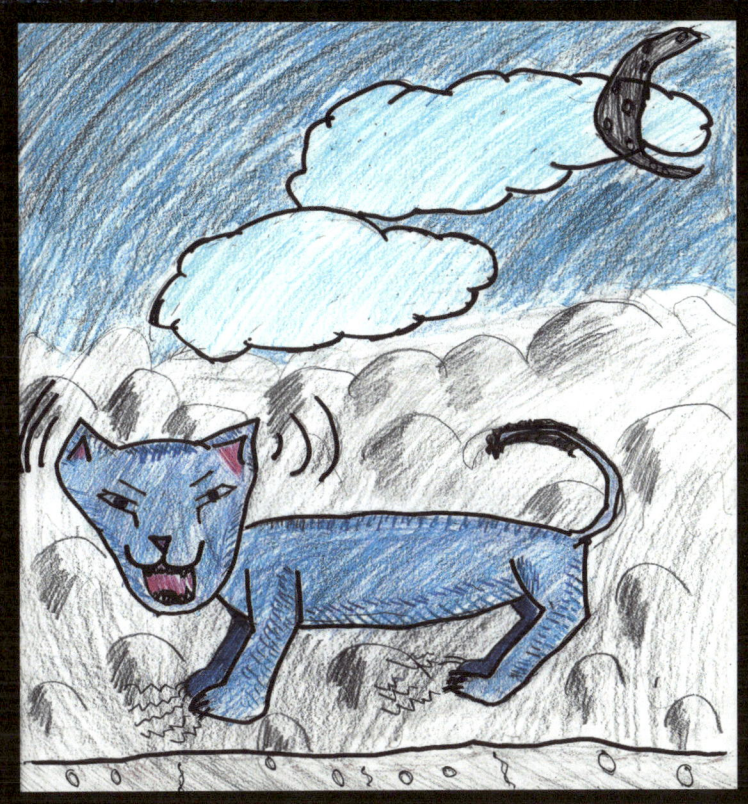

The Night Moon Panther is a good hunter at night and can dig into its prey. Its claws have an electrical shock that can stun its prey. This animal lives in rough, rocky mountains. If it sees its prey it climbs up and shocks the prey and sucks its blood when it's thirsty. This animal runs and can scream and make itself float off the ground so it can spot its prey. It eats rabbits, frogs, cats, and lizards with its sharp teeth. Its color can help it blend in at night so nothing can see it coming. All they get is their last chance to live!
Created by: Jasani Gladden

FISHENTATER

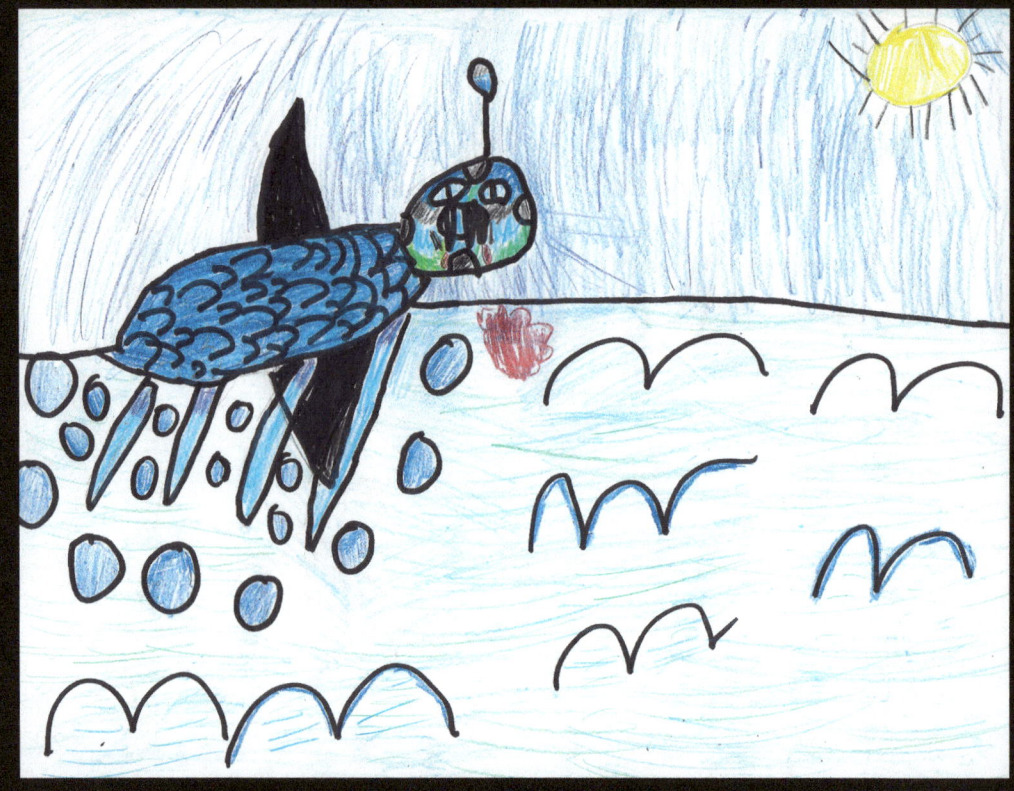

This is a Fishentater. It lives in the water. It has gills and a big hole in the middle so it can live inside the ocean. It can turn into something that goes up out of the water. It is really deadly and if a person eats it, they would die in five minutes.
It moves fast! It uses its legs to go really fast to catch its prey. It eats the Slime-Blade.

Created by: Zaniah Bracey

SLIME-BLADE

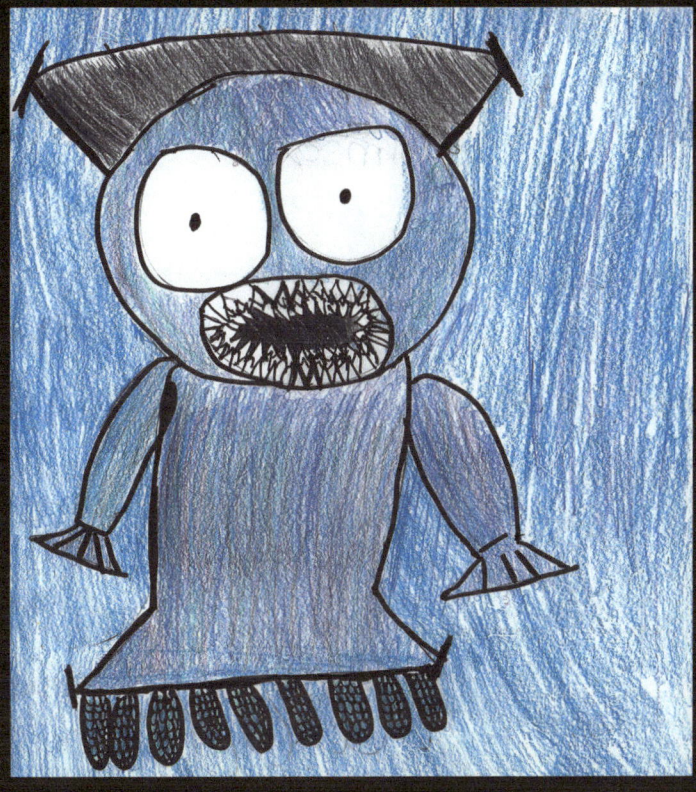

The Slime-Blade lives in the wet, moist sea. It lives in any water except for swamps, ponds, and lakes. This creature swims at almost 100 miles per hour and can go 3,000 feet deep into the ocean. It has zero bones except for its teeth. The animal is silver. Its luminous tail slashes at its prey. It eats crabs and sharks. Its slimy nine legs help it move inside the blue ocean. It has a metal blade on its head to hit its prey.
Created by: Sariaya Johnson

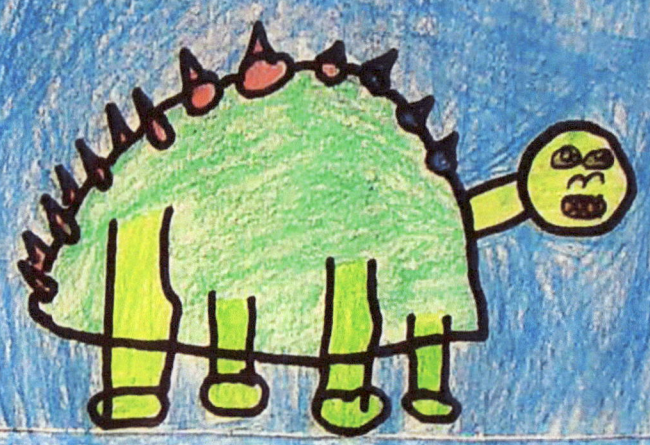

**Alternate Cover Designed By:
Daomi Chevannes**

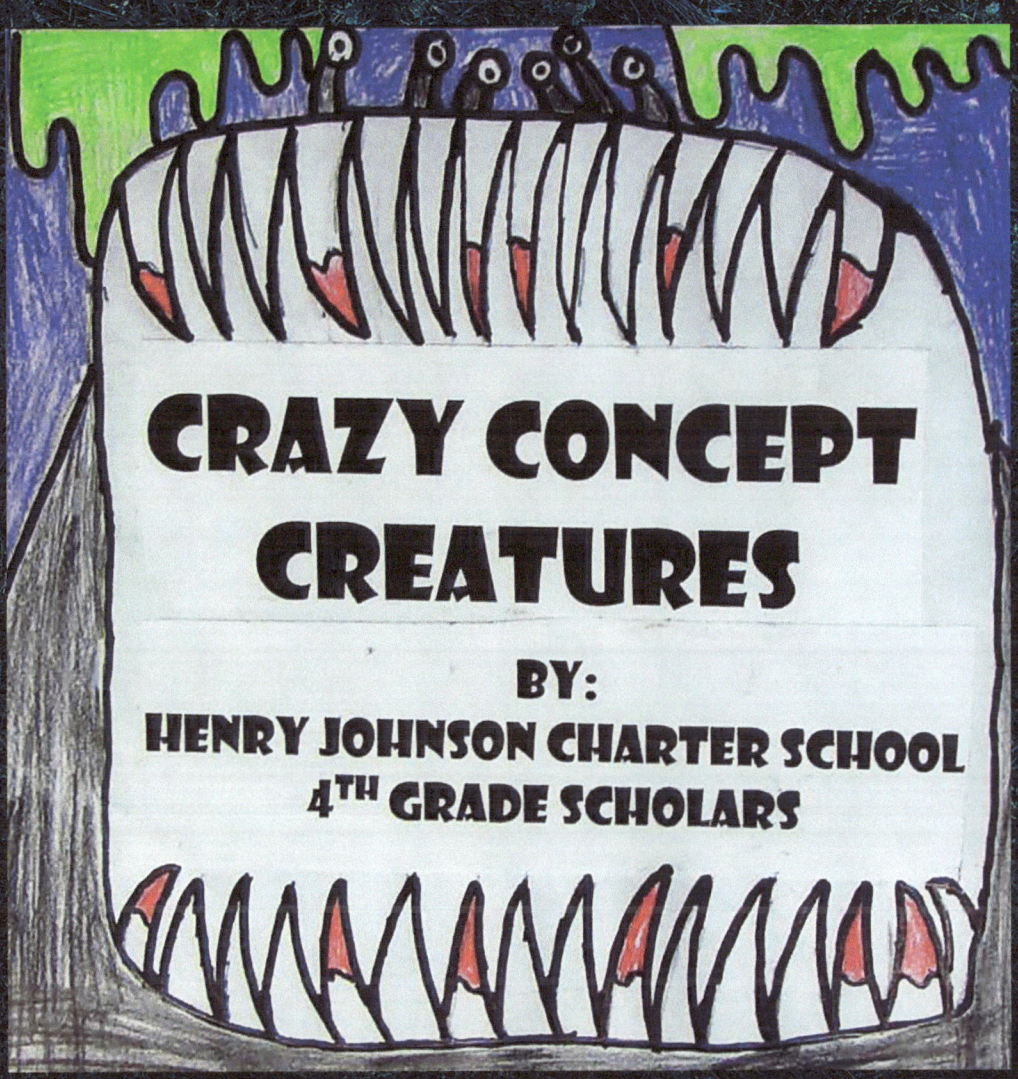

Alternate Cover Designed By:
Elijah Olarinde

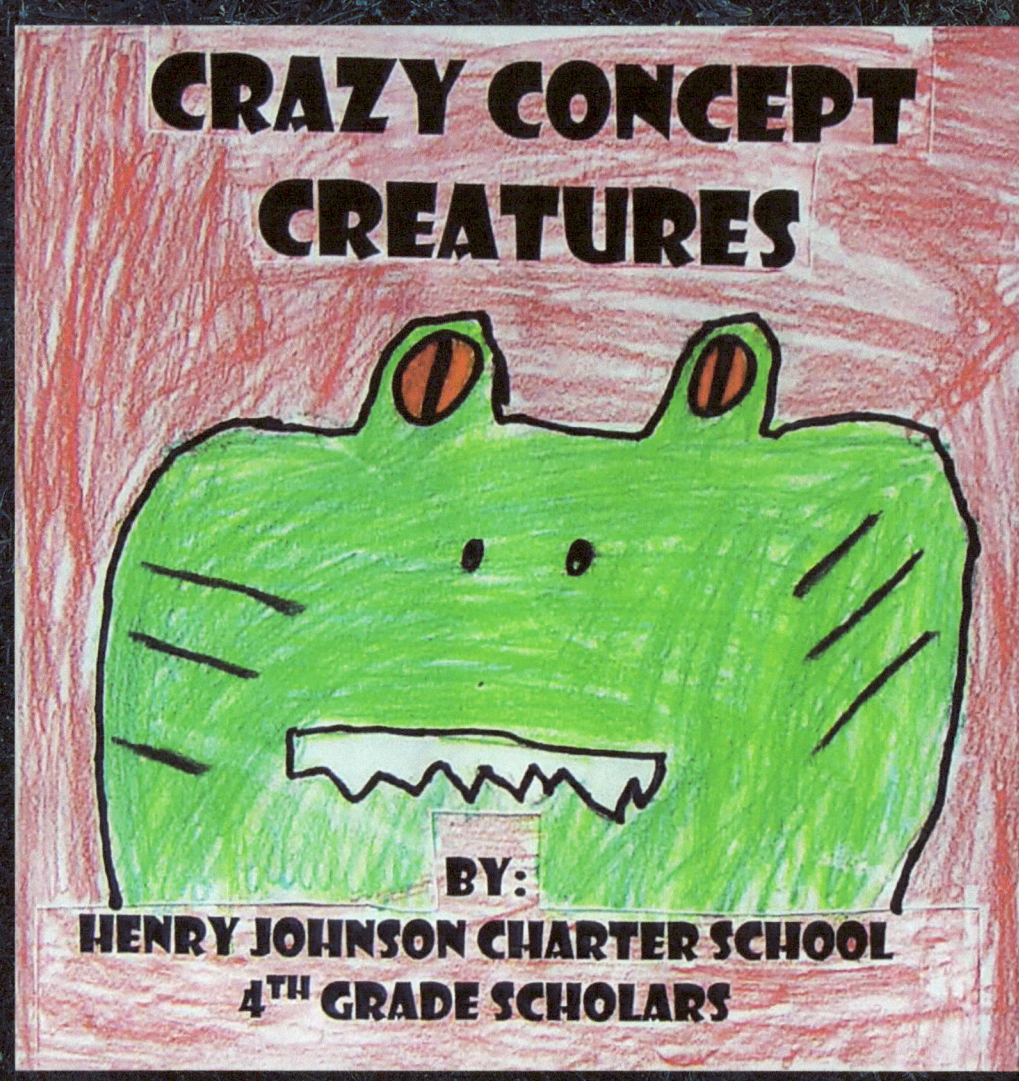

**Alternate Cover Designed By:
Damani Wilson-Anderson**

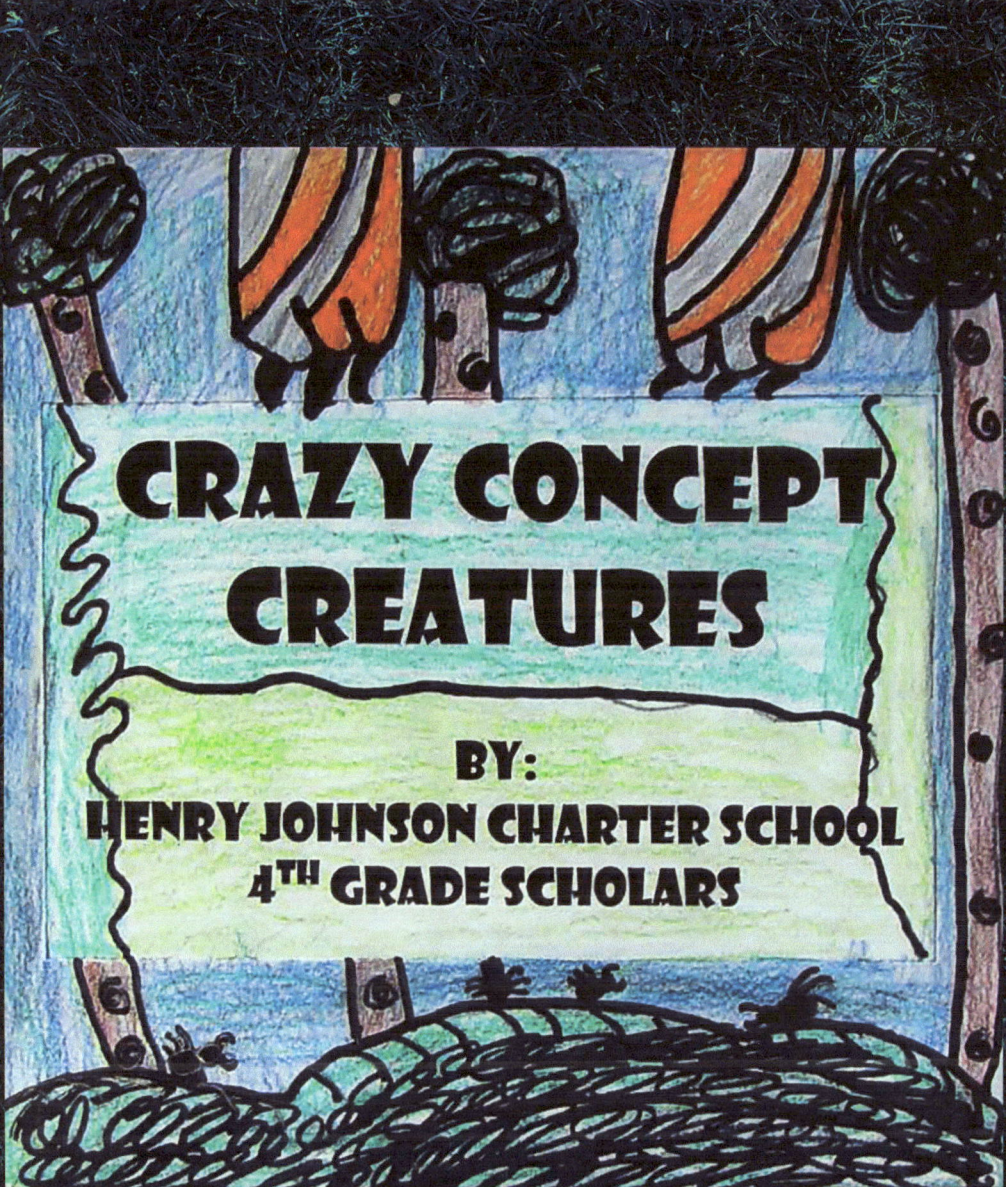

www.ingramcontent.com/pod-product-compliance
Lightning Source LLC
Chambersburg PA
CBHW040259220526
45473CB00002B/530